Black Beauty Activity Book

By David E. Cutts

Illustrated by Monika Popowitz

Watermill Press

10 9 8 7 6 5 4

When I was a young colt, I ran by my mother's side in a lovely...

Read each word and write its opposite. Then read down the circled letters to complete the sentence.

cool   _ _ _ O

worst   O _ _

subtract   O _ _

hot   _ _ _ O

come   _ O

fast   _ _ _ O

answer: page 52

2

My first owner was patient and gentle when he broke me in, so I was not afraid.

To find out what a horse is taught when it is being broken in, cross out the following letters:

F * G * H * M * P * U

T	O	M	W	E	G	A	R
F	A	B	U	R	I	G	D
L	H	E	A	P	N	D	U
S	A	G	D	D	F	L	E
H	A	N	P	D	T	F	O
C	H	A	R	M	R	Y	U
A	R	M	I	D	P	E	R

Then enter the remaining letters on the lines below.

— —   — — — —   — —   — — — — — —

— — —   — — — — — —   — — —

— —   — — — — —   —

— — — — —.

answer: page 52

When I was four years old, I was sold to

$\overline{F}\ \overline{D}\ \overline{H}\ \overline{V}\ \overline{E}\ \overline{R}\quad \overline{T}\ \overline{B}\ \overline{E}\ \overline{Q}\ \overline{B}\ \overline{A}$.

His wife said, "You could call him

$\overline{O}\ \overline{Y}\ \overline{N}\ \overline{P}\ \overline{X}\ \overline{O}\ \overline{V}\ \overline{E}\ \overline{Q}$."

A = N	
B = O	
C = P	
D = Q	
E = R	
F = S	
G = T	
H = U	
I = V	
J = W	
K = X	
L = Y	
M = Z	

But the squire said, "No. He is too handsome for that." Then she said, "Let's call him

$\overline{O}\ \overline{Y}\ \overline{N}\ \overline{P}\ \overline{X}$

$\overline{O}\ \overline{R}\ \overline{N}\ \overline{H}\ \overline{G}\ \overline{L}$."

Use the code to fill in the blanks.

answer: page 53

I shared a stable with a chestnut mare.

To find out what her name was, follow the path through the maze.

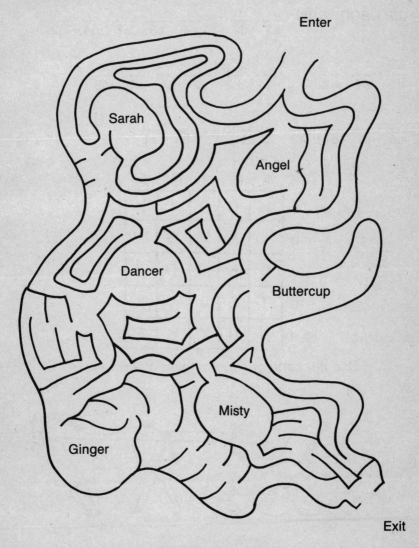

Enter

Sarah

Angel

Dancer

Buttercup

Ginger

Misty

Exit

answer: page 53

The coachman's name was John Manley.
One day he hitched me to a one-horse
carriage, and __ __ __ __ __ __ __
             b5 d2 c4 c5 a2 d4 d2

__ __ __ __ __ __ __ __ __
d1 a1 d2 e4 c3 e2 a4 c5 d2

__ __ __ __ __ __ __ __ .
a4 e1 d1 a2 d1 a2 b5 e1

	1	2	3	4	5
a	H	O	B	I	P
b	L	A	M	G	W
c	C	K	Q	D	R
d	T	E	J	V	X
e	N	U	Y	S	F

Use the code grid to complete the message.

answer: page 53

On the way home the <u>river</u> had <u>risen</u> so high that the middle of the <u>bridge</u> was under water. I knew <u>something</u> was <u>wrong</u>, and <u>I refused</u> to <u>cross</u>.

Can you fit the underlined words into the puzzle below?

answer: page 53

The toll keeper cried out from the other side,

"_____ _____ _____ _____!

OUY   NCOANT   SROCS   EHRE

_____ _____ _____ _____ _____

HET   DIMLED   FO   HTE   DEGRIB

_____ _____ _____!"

SI   ESHAWD   TOU

Unscramble the letters
and write the correct words
on the lines to complete
the sentences.

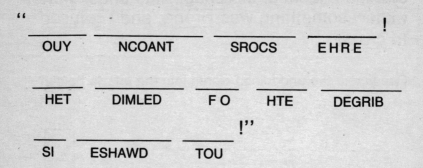

answer: page 54

8

When we finally arrived home, my master said,"If it had not been for Black Beauty we would have been swept away in the river!"

The underlined words above have been hidden in the puzzle below. Can you find and circle them?

B	A	R	I	V	E	R	S
T	B	L	A	C	K	I	O
S	E	L	S	W	E	P	T
W	A	I	F	O	A	Y	A
W	U	I	N	U	L	Y	R
H	T	O	D	L	M	E	R
E	Y	H	A	D	T	R	I
N	A	N	O	S	O	H	V
B	I	M	A	M	A	T	E
F	O	M	Y	E	E	S	D

answer: page 54

One day, my master and mistress went on a long trip. Ginger and I pulled the carriage

all day. At dusk __ __ __ __ __ __ __ __ __

__ __ __ __ __ __ __ __ .

Cross out every other letter, moving clockwise from the arrow. Then write the remaining letters on the lines above.

answer: page 54

10

That night, a fire broke out in the stable.
Ginger and I were

$\overline{}$ $\overline{}$ $\overline{}$ $\overline{}$ $\overline{}$ $\overline{}$ $\overline{}$ $\overline{}$ $\overline{}$ $\overline{}$ $\overline{}$
 1   2   3   4   5   6   7   8   9 10 11

and led out to safety.

Read each word and write its opposite. Then write the
first letter of each answer in each numbered line above.

1. good   _____   6. near   _____

2. talk   _____   7. in   _____

3. out   _____   8. cry   _____

4. yes   _____   9. wet   _____

5. up   _____   10. begin   _____

                                 11. alive   _____

answer: page 54

One night, my mistress was very ill. John climbed into my saddle.

Follow the path through the maze to find out where we went.

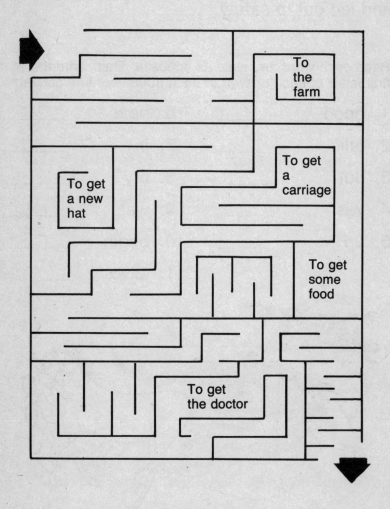

To
the
farm

To get
a
carriage

To get
a new
hat

To get
some
food

To get
the doctor

answer: page 55

12

Although I was already tired, I had to carry the

_____   _____   _____
codort   cbak   ot

_____   _____   _____.
elph   ym   strimses

_____   _____   _____
ew   riravde   ni

_____   _____   _____
eht   kinc   fo

_____.
item

Unscramble each word and write it on the line above.

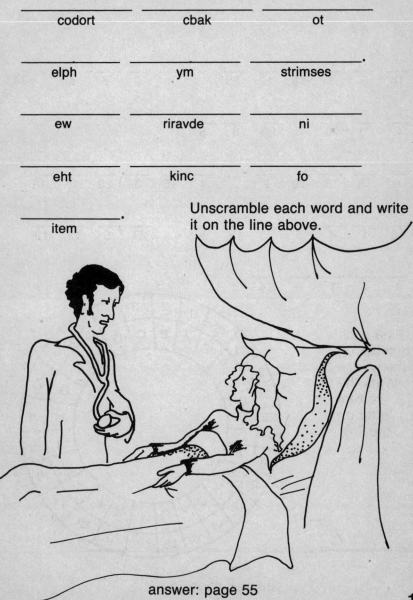

answer: page 55

13

That night, I $\underline{\text{C}}$ $\underline{\text{A}}$ $\underline{\text{U}}$ $\underline{\text{G}}$ $\underline{\text{H}}$ $\underline{\text{T}}$ $\underline{\text{A}}$
3 1 21 7 8 20   1

$\underline{\text{C}}$ $\underline{\text{H}}$ $\underline{\text{I}}$ $\underline{\text{L}}$ $\underline{\text{L}}$ $\underline{\text{A}}$ $\underline{\text{N}}$ $\underline{\text{D}}$
3 8 9 12 12   1 14 4

$\underline{\text{N}}$ $\underline{\text{E}}$ $\underline{\text{A}}$ $\underline{\text{R}}$ $\underline{\text{L}}$ $\underline{\text{Y}}$ $\underline{\text{D}}$ $\underline{\text{I}}$ $\underline{\text{E}}$ $\underline{\text{D}}$.
14 5 1 18 12 25   4 9 5 4

$\underline{\text{B}}$ $\underline{\text{U}}$ $\underline{\text{T}}$ $\underline{\text{T}}$ $\underline{\text{H}}$ $\underline{\text{E}}$
2 21 20   20 8 5

$\underline{\text{H}}$ $\underline{\text{O}}$ $\underline{\text{R}}$ $\underline{\text{S}}$ $\underline{\text{E}}$ $\underline{\text{D}}$ $\underline{\text{O}}$ $\underline{\text{C}}$ $\underline{\text{T}}$ $\underline{\text{O}}$ $\underline{\text{R}}$
8 15 18 19 5   4 15 3 20 15 18

$\underline{\text{M}}$ $\underline{\text{A}}$ $\underline{\text{D}}$ $\underline{\text{E}}$ $\underline{\text{M}}$ $\underline{\text{E}}$ $\underline{\text{W}}$ $\underline{\text{E}}$ $\underline{\text{L}}$ $\underline{\text{L}}$
13 1 4 5   13 5   23 5 12 12

$\underline{\text{A}}$ $\underline{\text{G}}$ $\underline{\text{A}}$ $\underline{\text{I}}$ $\underline{\text{N}}$.
1 7 1 9 14

Find each number on the wheel. Write the correct letter on the line.

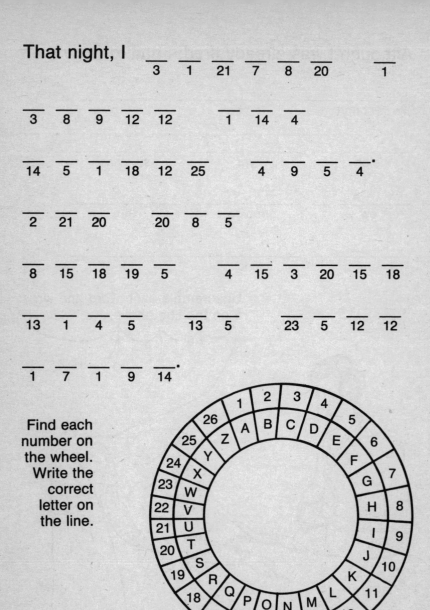

answer: page 55

In time, Squire Gordon moved away.

To find out what happened to Ginger and me, follow the correct spelling of my name.

FOR SALE

B L A C K

T U A E B E A U T Y

Y

We were sold.

We went with them.

We ran away.

answer: page 55

Our new mistress made us wear "bearing reins" to keep our heads up high. They were fashionable but very

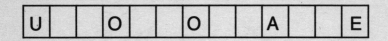

U		O		O		A		E

Place the following consonants in the boxes above to complete the word.

B C F L M N R T

answer: page 56

One day, as the bearing reins were being shortened again, Ginger reared up and started kicking. After that

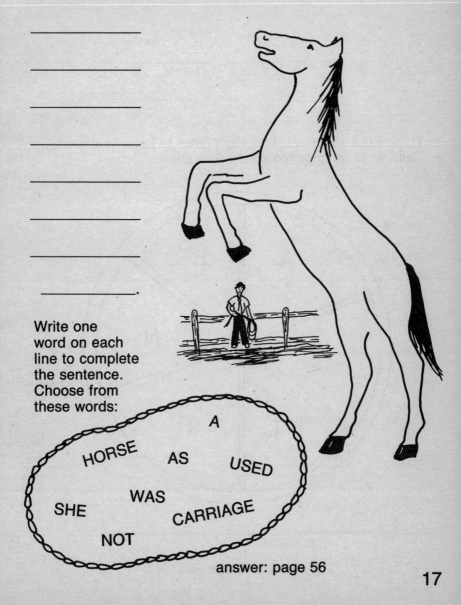

_____

_____

_____

_____

_____

_____

_____.

Write one word on each line to complete the sentence. Choose from these words:

A

HORSE   AS   USED

WAS

SHE   CARRIAGE

NOT

answer: page 56

17

In the spring, my owners went to London, and I stayed in the country, where I was ridden every day by

$$\overline{\quad}\ \overline{\quad}\ \overline{\quad}\ \overline{\quad}\qquad \overline{\quad}\ \overline{\quad}\ \overline{\quad}\ \overline{\quad}$$
E   D   A   N   D   Y   Y   L

To find out who rode, find each letter in the wheel below. Then write its opposite on the line above.

answer: page 56

One day, she rode Lizzie instead of me.
Her cousin said Lizzie was too nervous,

a2 d3 d2   c1 a1 a4 d4

a1 c3 c3 b1   a4 b4 a4   c3 c4 d2

a3 b3 a1 c3 b2 b1   b3 b1 d1

c2 b4 c3 a4.

Find the row and column. Write the correct letter on each line to finish the sentence.

	1	2	3	4
a	A	B	C	D
b	E	G	H	I
c	L	M	N	O
d	R	T	U	Y

answer: page 56

Something frightened Lizzie, who galloped off.

To find out what happened next, find the path through the maze. Write the correct words on the lines below.

— — — —   — — — —   — — — — —

— —   — — — —   — — — —

— — — —.

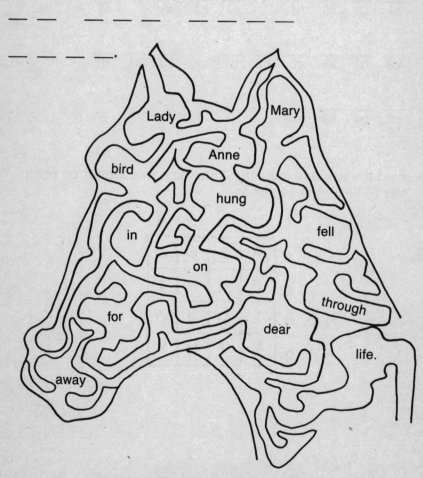

answer: page 57

Later, Lady Anne would ride no other horse
except me.

How long will it take you to fit all the above words into
the puzzle below?

One has been
done for you.

answer: page 57

Our head groom, Reuben Smith, was a careless fellow. One night a terrible thing happened.

Follow the path through the maze.

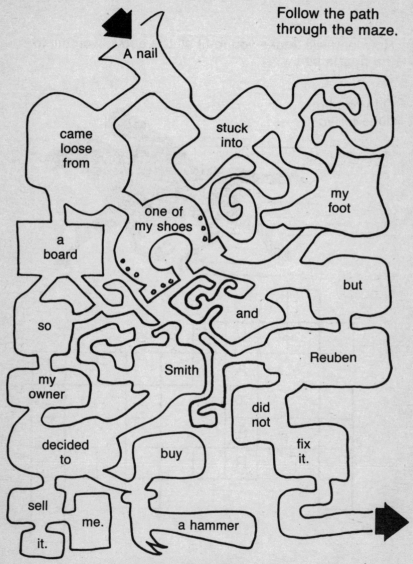

answer: page 57

22

As he rode me home, my loose shoe came off and I stumbled and fell to my knees.

Unscramble the letters to spell the words that tell what happened.

EBRUNE   TSMIH

SAW   HOWTRN   OT

SIH   HEADT .

answer: page 57

After that, my knees were scarred.

Cross out the odd letters in odd-numbered rows, and the even letters in even-numbered rows. Then write the remaining letters on the lines below.

1	A	S	L	O	W	M	A	Y	A	M	I
2	A	R	S	I	T	L	E	E	R	T	S
3	P	O	L	L	S	D	O	M	E	E	N
4	T	O	O	T	A	L	L	E	I	S	V
5	R	E	A	R	A	Y	S	S	O	T	H
6	A	R	B	I	L	A	E	D	W	O	H
7	W	E	A	R	E	E	N	H	O	O	T
8	R	O	S	E	E	N	S	E	W	E	E
9	O	R	M	E	P	O	W	F	I	F	I
10	E	R	R	O	E	N	D	O	F	F	O
11	A	R	E	H	O	I	D	R	Y	E	S

— —   — —   — — — — — — —   — — — —

— —   — —   —   — — — — —

— — — — — —,   — — — — —

— — — — — —   — — — —

— — — — — — —   — — —   — — — —.

answer: page 58

24

Some of the people who rented me did not know anything about horses. So I was not _____ well.

Form a word on each row, using only the letters from the row above.

Then unscramble the circled letters to spell a word that completes the sentence above.

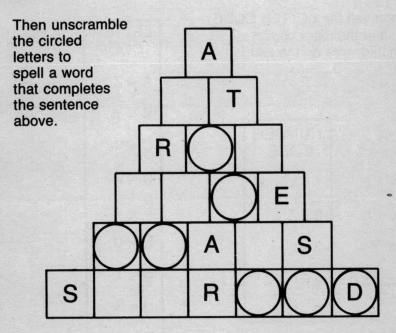

scrambled letters _ _ _ _ _ _ _

unscrambled word _ _ _ _ _ _ _

answer: page 58

My next owner had never owned a horse before, but he bought the best food for me.

His name was Mr. $\underline{}_{1}\ \underline{}_{2}\ \underline{}_{3}\ \underline{}_{4}\ \underline{}_{5}.$

To complete the owner's name, first use the NUMBER CODE to find a secret letter.

Then use the LETTER CODE to find the letter you should write on the line.

NUMBER CODE
1 = Y
2 = Z
3 = I
4 = I
5 = B

LETTER CODE
A = Z
B = Y
C = X
D = W
E = V
F = U
G = T
H = S
I = R
J = Q
K = P
L = O
M = N

answer: page 58

The groom stole my oats and did not give me enough to eat. He was arrested, and another groom was hired.

Find the path through the maze.

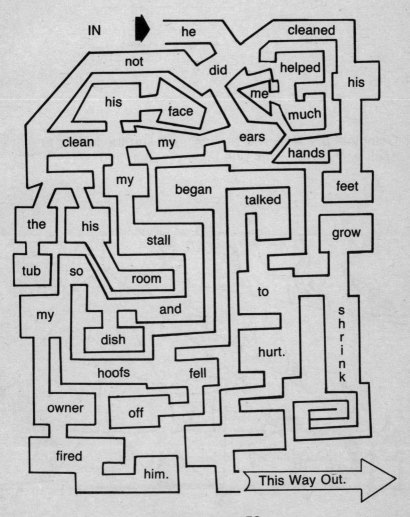

answer: page 58

Mr. Barry decided that being a horse owner was too much trouble, so I was sold at a

RSHOE   __ __ __ __ __

ARIF   __ __ __ __.

Complete the sentence by unscrambling the letters to spell each word. Print one letter on each line.

answer: page 59

My new owner had me pull his cab through the London streets.

To find out his name, cross out *one* letter and skip one. Then cross out *two* letters and skip one. Then cross out *three* letters and skip one. Continue from left to right until you have crossed out eleven and skipped one.

A	J	U	M	E	T	H
B	R	O	W	N	O	R
C	F	U	N	N	Y	O
D	R	O	O	L	B	Y
E	R	A	S	E	M	A
F	U	E	L	U	P	S
G	R	E	A	T	E	R
H	I	K	E	K	A	P
I	N	D	I	A	N	S
J	E	S	T	E	R	A
K	I	N	G	A	U	R

Finally print the remaining letters in the spaces below.

— — — — —   — — — — — —

answer: page 59

One Sunday morning, Jerry hitched me to a light carriage for a trip to the country.

To find out what kind
of a person Jerry was,
fill in each section
of the puzzle that
contains a dot.

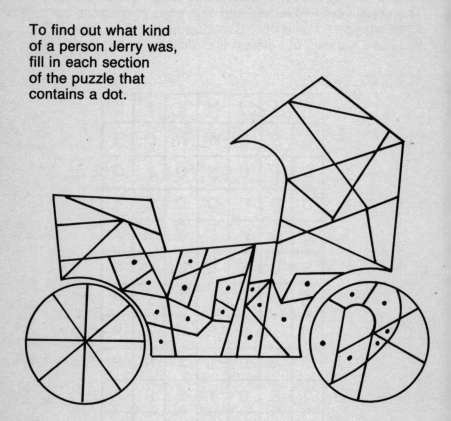

answer: page 59

When we arrived, he took off my harness so I could roll in the meadow.

All the words in this sentence are hidden in the puzzle below. Can you find them?

B	W	Y	T	H	M	D	I
M	H	A	R	N	E	S	S
Y	E	X	T	V	S	R	C
W	N	A	I	H	Z	O	O
I	Q	R	D	F	E	L	U
N	R	O	F	O	P	L	L
A	T	O	O	K	W	E	D

answer: page 59

Jerry was always doing favors for people. Once he took a young woman and her sick baby to the hospital for free because

$\overline{\text{V}-3}$ $\overline{\text{G}+1}$ $\overline{\text{A}+4}$ $\quad$ $\overline{\text{H}-4}$ $\overline{\text{H}+1}$ $\overline{\text{J}-6}$

$\overline{\text{Q}-3}$ $\overline{\text{N}+1}$ $\overline{\text{X}-4}$ $\quad$ $\overline{\text{D}+4}$ $\overline{\text{C}-2}$ $\overline{\text{Z}-4}$ $\overline{\text{B}+3}$

$\overline{\text{P}-3}$ $\overline{\text{Q}-2}$ $\overline{\text{J}+4}$ $\overline{\text{G}-2}$ $\overline{\text{Z}-1}$ $\quad$ $\overline{\text{A}+5}$ $\overline{\text{K}+4}$ $\overline{\text{Q}+1}$

$\overline{\text{A}+2}$ $\overline{\text{C}-2}$ $\overline{\text{D}-2}$ $\quad$ $\overline{\text{H}-2}$ $\overline{\text{D}-3}$ $\overline{\text{Q}+1}$ $\overline{\text{C}+2}$.

Use the code to solve the mystery message. Look below each blank line. You will see a letter, a plus or minus sign, and a number.

Start at the letter in the alphabet code and move the number of spaces shown.

(Plus is to the right; minus is to the left.)

ALPHABET CODE

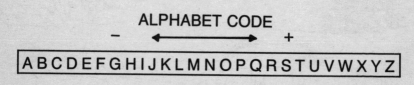

− ⟵——————⟶ +

A B C D E F G H I J K L M N O P Q R S T U V W X Y Z

answer: page 60

Follow the path through the city streets from the cab stand to the hospital.

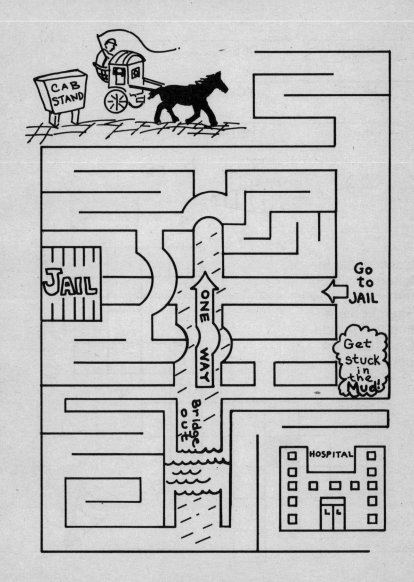

answer: page 60

On New Year's Eve, Jerry drove two men to a party.

_____ _____ _____ to
HEYT   DESAK   MIH

_____ _____ _____ to
MOCE   KCAB   RALTE

_____ _____ up.
IKPC   HETM

Unscramble the
letters to spell
the correct words.
Then fit them
into this puzzle.
One has been
done for you.

34

answer: page 60

But when <u>we</u> <u>showed</u> up, the <u>men</u> <u>kept</u> <u>us</u> <u>waiting</u> in the <u>cold</u> for <u>hours</u>.

Find the underlined words above in the maze below.

S	X	K	B	M	S	T	W
H	U	S	E	R	L	D	H
O	Z	M	U	P	L	B	E
W	R	O	E	O	T	U	N
E	H	W	C	N	Q	T	N
D	W	A	I	T	I	N	G

answer: page 60

Jerry had caught a chill.

Follow the right path through the maze to find out what happened.

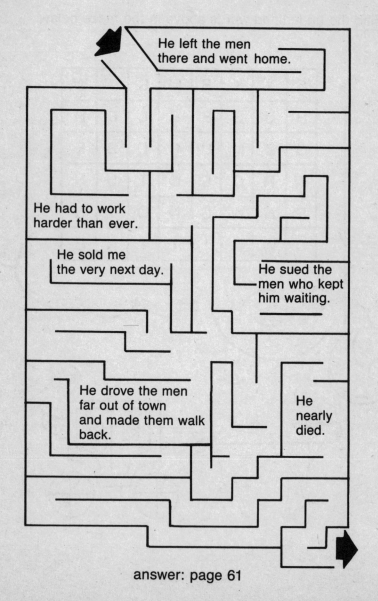

He left the men there and went home.

He had to work harder than ever.

He sold me the very next day.

He sued the men who kept him waiting.

He drove the men far out of town and made them walk back.

He nearly died.

answer: page 61

Because of his health, Jerry was not able to drive a cab any more.

Find the letters that appear in each box with a star. Moving from left to right, enter them on the lines below.

A	N	*S	W	E	R	T	*O	M	Y
G	*O	O	D	O	*N	E	A	R	*C
D	R	*E	S	S	F	*A	N	T	A
*G	O	L	D	*A	L	O	N	G	*I
A	*N	G	E	L	*I	N	O	*W	N
*A	S	K	*S	F	O	R	*S	A	D
F	*O	R	O	W	*L	S	B	E	*D

__ __   __ __ __ __ __   __ __ __ __ __

__   __ __ __   __ __ __ __ .

answer: page 61

I was next bought by a man who

$$\overline{12}\ \overline{16}\ \overline{9}\ \overline{7} \quad \overline{25}\ \overline{9} \quad \overline{1}\ \overline{16} \quad \overline{1}$$

$$\overline{5}\ \overline{1}\ \overline{18}\ \overline{14} \quad \overline{15}\ \overline{24}\ \overline{18}\ \overline{16}\ \overline{9}.$$

Use the code to complete the sentence.

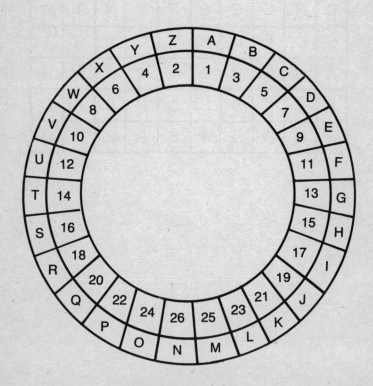

answer: page 61

The foreman kept piling boxes on. He said,

"— — — — — — , — —
14 15 9 18 9 16   26 24

— — — — —   — —
16 9 26 16 9   17 26

— — — — — —   — — —
25 1 21 17 26 13   14 8 24

— — — — —   — —
14 18 17 22 16   17 11

— — —   — — — —   — —.
24 26 9   8 17 23 23   7 24

Use the code
on page 38 to
find out what he said.

answer: page 61

My next owner was the meanest man I ever met. His name was Nicholas

$$\overline{}_{14} \quad \text{K} \quad \overline{}_{28} \quad \overline{}_{3} \quad \overline{}_{39} \quad \overline{}_{42} \quad \overline{}_{32}$$

To find out Nicholas's last name, read the number under the first line. Then count the letters, beginning at the top of the page with "My next owner," until you come to that number. Write that letter on the line. Then, starting again with "My next owner," count up to the next number and so forth.

answer: page 62

He worked me so hard that I began to wish I would die. One day,

To complete the sentence, find the path through the maze.

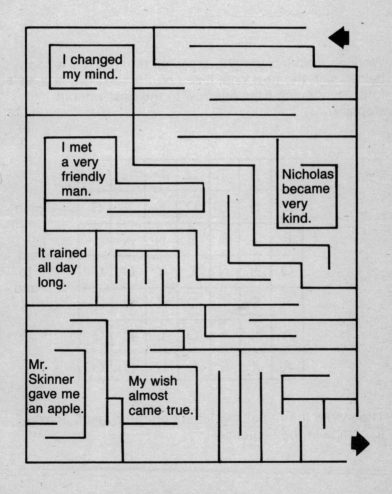

I changed my mind.

I met a very friendly man.

Nicholas became very kind.

It rained all day long.

Mr. Skinner gave me an apple.

My wish almost came true.

answer: page 62

I was pulling a cab that was so heavily loaded that

— — — — — — — — — —

— — — — — —.

Working from left to right, cross off the first two letters below, skip the next one, cross off the next two and so forth, continuing from one row to the next without stopping.

A	R	T	N	P	H	O
I	E	L	D	S	K	S
P	T	R	R	N	A	I
O	N	N	L	Y	G	O
P	S	T	O	S	Q	Z
A	N	I	G	L	E	G
A	X	E	L	R	D	O

Then write the remaining letters on the spaces above to complete the sentence.

answer: page 62

I did the best I could, but the load was too heavy to pull. My feet slipped.

Starting at the arrow and moving clockwise, cross out the first letter, then every other one.

Write the remaining letters on the lines.

—   — — — —   — —

— — —   — — — — — —.

answer: page 62

The doctors said I needed plenty of rest before I could work again. So Skinner decided to

— — — —   — —.

Color in the shapes that do not have a dot.

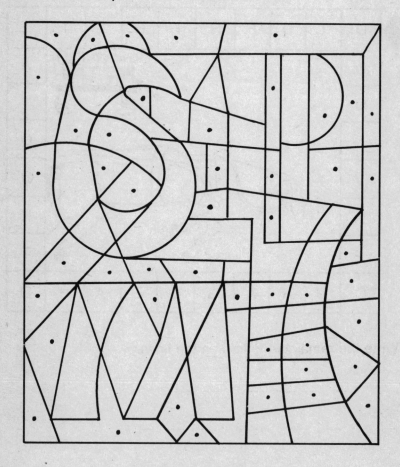

answer: page 63

I was bought by a gentleman farmer, whose grandson said

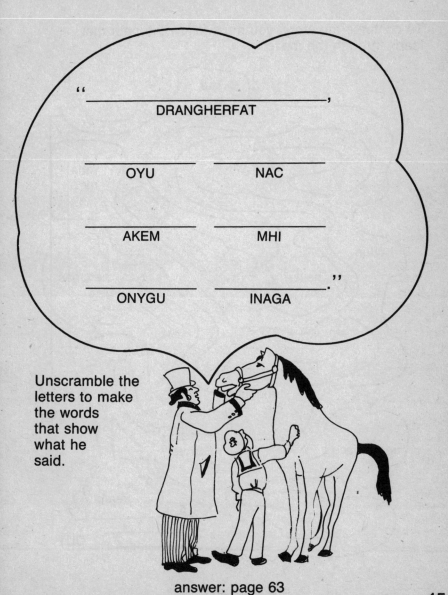

"_____,
　　　　DRANGHERFAT

_____　　_____
　　　OYU　　　　　　　　NAC

_____　　_____
　　　AKEM　　　　　　　　MHI

_____　　_____."
　　　ONYGU　　　　　　　INAGA

Unscramble the letters to make the words that show what he said.

answer: page 63

At their farm in the country, I was put into a large meadow.

To continue the story, you must follow the path that leads through the maze.

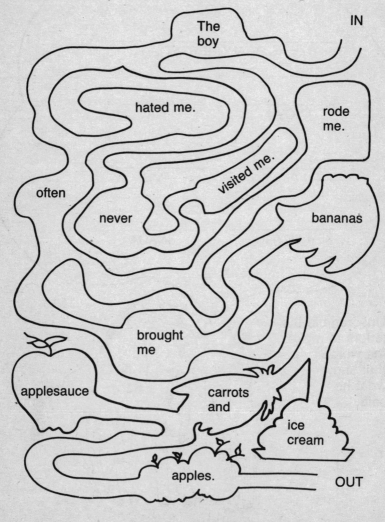

answer: page 63

Over the winter, my legs grew strong again.

$\overline{O}\ \overline{L}$ $\overline{F}\ \overline{C}\ \overline{E}\ \overline{V}\ \overline{A}\ \overline{T}\text{'}\ \overline{V}$

$\overline{S}\ \overline{R}\ \overline{Y}\ \overline{G}$ $\overline{L}\ \overline{B}\ \overline{H}\ \overline{A}\ \overline{T}\ \overline{R}\ \overline{E}$

$\overline{G}\ \overline{U}\ \overline{N}\ \overline{A}$ $\overline{V}$ $\overline{U}\ \overline{N}\ \overline{Q}$

$\overline{V}\ \overline{A}$ $\overline{L}\ \overline{R}\ \overline{N}\ \overline{E}\ \overline{F}.$

A = N	
B = O	
C = P	**Use the code to solve the secret message.**
D = Q	
E = R	
F = S	
G = T	
H = U	
I = V	
J = W	
K = X	
L = Y	
M = Z	

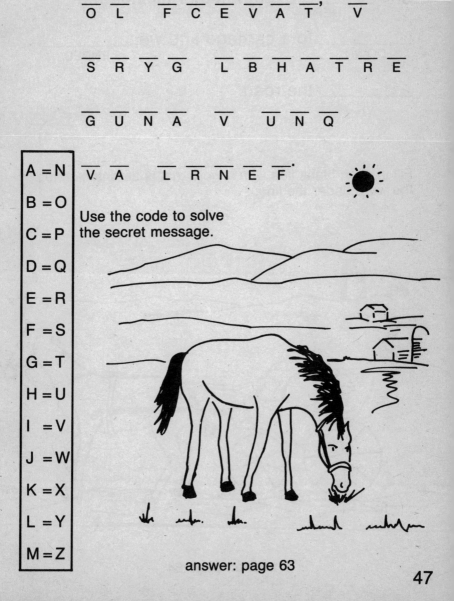

answer: page 63

One _____ _____ the _____
WINTER   NIGHT   GIRL

and _____ grandfather hitched me
HER

_____ to a carriage and we _____
DOWN   ENDED

_____ the road.
UP

Fill in each blank line with a word that is an antonym for the word under the line.

answer: page 64

We stopped at a fine house and three ladies looked me over. One of them said,

"W_ W_L L _S_
H_M F_R _F_W
D_YS, _ND _F
H_ _S G__D W_
W_LL B_Y H_M."

Fill in the blanks with the vowels
A-E-I-O-U
to complete the sentence.

answer: page 64

Their coachman was my old stable boy from Squire Gordon's. He looked at me closely and said,

"_____ _____, is

_____ _____ _____?"

Fill in the blanks with words from those listed below.
Then fit them into the puzzle.

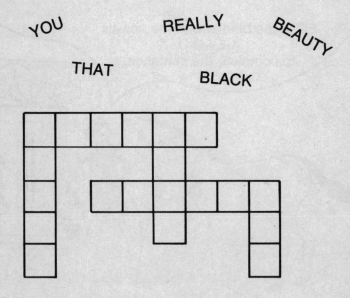

YOU   REALLY   BEAUTY

THAT   BLACK

answer: page 64

They bought me and gave me a good home.
And at last I am

_ _ _ _ _.

Write the opposites:

Goodbye ◯ _ _ _ _

None ◯ _ _

Push ◯ _ _ _

Rich ◯ _ _ _

No ◯ _ _

Now write the circled letters in the spaces to complete the sentence.

answer: page 64

answer for page 2

cool   <u>W</u>   <u>A</u>   <u>R</u>   Ⓜ

worst   <u>B</u>   Ⓔ   <u>S</u>   <u>T</u>

subtract   Ⓐ   <u>D</u>   <u>D</u>

hot   <u>C</u>   <u>O</u>   <u>L</u>   Ⓓ

come   <u>G</u>   Ⓞ

fast   <u>S</u>   <u>L</u>   <u>O</u>   Ⓦ

answer for page 3

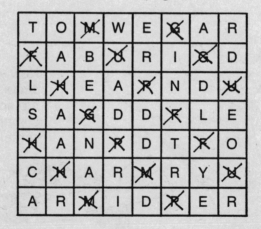

<u>T</u> <u>O</u>   <u>W</u> <u>E</u> <u>A</u> <u>R</u>   <u>A</u>   <u>B</u> <u>R</u> <u>I</u> <u>D</u> <u>L</u> <u>E</u>
<u>A</u> <u>N</u> <u>D</u>   <u>S</u> <u>A</u> <u>D</u> <u>D</u> <u>L</u> <u>E</u>   <u>A</u> <u>N</u> <u>D</u>
<u>T</u> <u>O</u>   <u>C</u> <u>A</u> <u>R</u> <u>R</u> <u>Y</u>   <u>A</u>
<u>R</u> <u>I</u> <u>D</u> <u>E</u> <u>R</u>.

answer for page 4

$$\underset{F}{S}\ \underset{D}{Q}\ \underset{H}{U}\ \underset{V}{I}\ \underset{E}{R}\ \underset{R}{E}\qquad \underset{T}{G}\ \underset{B}{O}\ \underset{E}{R}\ \underset{Q}{D}\ \underset{B}{O}\ \underset{A}{N}.$$

$$\underset{O}{B}\ \underset{Y}{L}\ \underset{N}{A}\ \underset{P}{C}\ \underset{X}{K}\ \underset{O}{B}\ \underset{V}{I}\ \underset{E}{R}\ \underset{Q}{D}."$$

$$\underset{O}{B}\ \underset{Y}{L}\ \underset{N}{A}\ \underset{P}{C}\ \underset{X}{K}$$

$$\underset{O}{B}\ \underset{R}{E}\ \underset{N}{A}\ \underset{H}{U}\ \underset{G}{T}\ \underset{L}{Y}."$$

answer for page 5

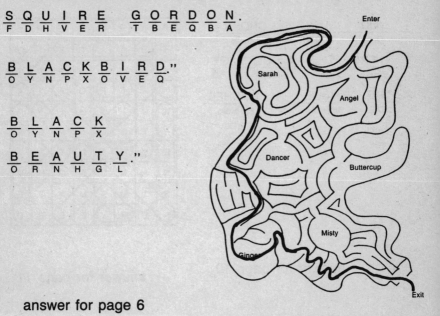

answer for page 6

$$\underset{b5}{w}\ \underset{d2}{e}\qquad \underset{c4}{d}\ \underset{c5}{r}\ \underset{a2}{o}\ \underset{d4}{v}\ \underset{d2}{e}$$

$$\underset{d1}{t}\ \underset{a1}{h}\ \underset{d2}{e}\qquad \underset{e4}{s}\ \underset{c3}{q}\ \underset{e2}{u}\ \underset{a4}{i}\ \underset{c5}{r}\ \underset{d2}{e}$$

$$\underset{a4}{i}\ \underset{e1}{n}\ \underset{d1}{t}\ \underset{a2}{o}\qquad \underset{d1}{t}\ \underset{a2}{o}\ \underset{b5}{w}\ \underset{e1}{n}.$$

answer for page 7

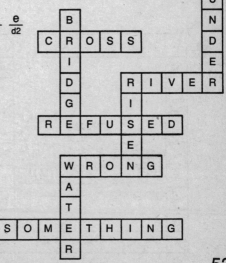

53

answer for page 8

" <u>YOU</u> <u>CANNOT</u> <u>CROSS</u>
OUY   NCOANT   SROCS

<u>HERE</u>! <u>THE</u> <u>MIDDLE</u> <u>OF</u>
EHRE   HET   DIMLED   FO

<u>THE</u> <u>BRIDGE</u> <u>IS</u> <u>WASHED</u>
HTE   DEGRIB   SI   ESHAWD

<u>OUT</u> !"
TOU

answer for page 9

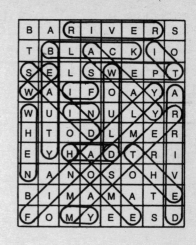

answer for page 10

<u>W E</u> <u>S T O P P E D</u>

<u>A T</u> <u>A</u> <u>H O T E L</u>.

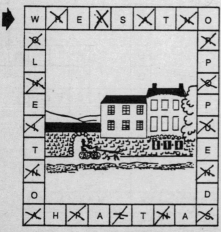

answer for page 11

<u>B</u> <u>L</u> <u>I</u> <u>N</u> <u>D</u> -
1   2   3   4   5

<u>F</u> <u>O</u> <u>L</u> <u>D</u> <u>E</u> <u>D</u>
6   7   8   9   10 11

1. good   <u>bad</u>
2. talk   <u>listen</u>
3. out   <u>in</u>
4. yes   <u>no</u>
5. up   <u>down</u>
6. near   <u>far</u>
7. in   <u>out</u>
8. cry   <u>laugh</u>
9. wet   <u>dry</u>
10. begin <u>end</u>
11. alive <u>dead</u>

answer for page 12

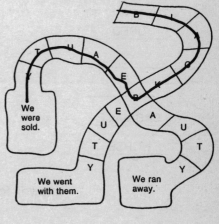

(maze diagram with labels: "To the farm", "To get a carriage", "To get a new hat", "To get some food", "To get the doctor")

answer for page 13

doctor	back	to
codort	cbak	ot

help	my	mistress .
elph	ym	strimses

we	arrived	in
ew	riravde	ni

the	nick	of
eht	kinc	fo

time .
item

answer for page 15

(path diagram: "We were sold." / "We went with them." / "We ran away.")

answer for page 14

I $\underset{3}{C}$ $\underset{1}{A}$ $\underset{21}{U}$ $\underset{7}{G}$ $\underset{8}{H}$ $\underset{20}{T}$ $\underset{1}{A}$

$\underset{3}{C}$ $\underset{8}{H}$ $\underset{9}{I}$ $\underset{12}{L}$ $\underset{12}{L}$ $\underset{1}{A}$ $\underset{14}{N}$ $\underset{4}{D}$

$\underset{14}{N}$ $\underset{5}{E}$ $\underset{1}{A}$ $\underset{18}{R}$ $\underset{12}{L}$ $\underset{25}{Y}$ $\underset{4}{D}$ $\underset{9}{I}$ $\underset{5}{E}$ $\underset{4}{D}$.

$\underset{2}{B}$ $\underset{21}{U}$ $\underset{20}{T}$ $\underset{20}{T}$ $\underset{8}{H}$ $\underset{5}{E}$

$\underset{8}{H}$ $\underset{15}{O}$ $\underset{18}{R}$ $\underset{19}{S}$ $\underset{5}{E}$ $\underset{4}{D}$ $\underset{15}{O}$ $\underset{3}{C}$ $\underset{20}{T}$ $\underset{15}{O}$ $\underset{18}{R}$

$\underset{13}{M}$ $\underset{1}{A}$ $\underset{4}{D}$ $\underset{5}{E}$ $\underset{13}{M}$ $\underset{5}{E}$ $\underset{23}{W}$ $\underset{5}{E}$ $\underset{12}{L}$ $\underset{12}{L}$

$\underset{1}{A}$ $\underset{7}{G}$ $\underset{1}{A}$ $\underset{9}{I}$ $\underset{14}{N}$.

55

answer for page 16

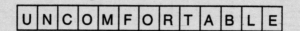

U N C O M F O R T A B L E

answer for page 17

SHE

WAS

NOT

USED

AS

A

CARRIAGE

HORSE .

answer for page 18

$$\frac{L}{E} \frac{A}{D} \frac{D}{A} \frac{Y}{N} \qquad \frac{A}{D} \frac{N}{Y} \frac{N}{Y} \frac{E}{L}$$

answer for page 19

$$\frac{B}{a2} \frac{U}{d3} \frac{T}{d2} \qquad \frac{L}{c1} \frac{A}{a1} \frac{D}{a4} \frac{Y}{d4}$$

$$\frac{A}{a1} \frac{N}{c3} \frac{N}{c3} \frac{E}{b1} \qquad \frac{D}{a4} \frac{I}{b4} \frac{D}{a4} \qquad \frac{N}{c3} \frac{O}{c4} \frac{T}{d2}$$

$$\frac{C}{a3} \frac{H}{b3} \frac{A}{a1} \frac{N}{c3} \frac{G}{b2} \frac{E}{b1} \qquad \frac{H}{b3} \frac{E}{b1} \frac{R}{d1}$$

$$\frac{M}{c2} \frac{I}{b4} \frac{N}{c3} \frac{D}{a4}.$$

answer for page 20

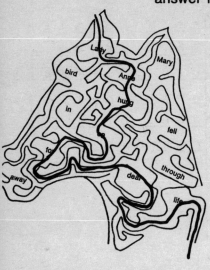

L A D Y   A N N E

H U N G   O N   F O R

D E A R   L I F E.

answer for page 21

	N								
W	O	U	L	D					
		A		H	O	R	S	E	
L		T			T			X	
A	N	N	E			H			C	
D		R	I	D	E		M	E	
Y					R			P	
								T	

answer for page 22

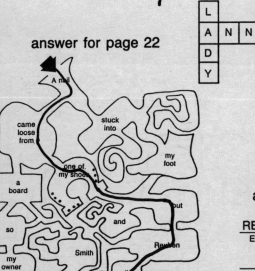

answer for page 23

REUBEN   SMITH
EBRUNE   TSMIH

WAS   THROWN
SAW   HOWTRN

TO   HIS
OT   SIH

DEATH .
HEADT

57

answer for page 24

	S		O		M		Y		M	
A		S		T		E		R		S
	O		L		D		M		E	
T		O	A		L		I		V
	E		R		Y		S		T	
A		B		L		E		W		H
	E		R		E		H		O	
R		S		E		S		W		E
	R		E		O		F		F	
E		R		E		D		F		O
	R		H		I		R		E	

S̲O̲ M̲Y̲ M̲A̲S̲T̲E̲R̲

S̲O̲L̲D̲ M̲E̲ T̲O̲ A̲

L̲I̲V̲E̲R̲Y̲ S̲T̲A̲B̲L̲E̲,

W̲H̲E̲R̲E̲ H̲O̲R̲S̲E̲S̲

W̲E̲R̲E̲ O̲F̲F̲E̲R̲E̲D̲

F̲O̲R̲ H̲I̲R̲E̲.

answer for page 25

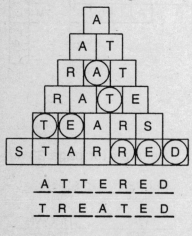

A̲ T̲ T̲ E̲ R̲ E̲ D̲

T̲ R̲ E̲ A̲ T̲ E̲ D̲

answer for page 26

B̲ A̲ R̲ R̲ Y̲.
1   2   3   4   5

answer for page 27

answer for page 28

H O R S E F A I R.

answer for page 29

J E R R Y

B A R K E R

answer for page 30

answer for page 31

answer for page 32

$\underset{V-3}{S}$ $\underset{G+1}{H}$ $\underset{A+4}{E}$ $\underset{H-4}{D}$ $\underset{H+1}{I}$ $\underset{J-6}{D}$

$\underset{Q-3}{N}$ $\underset{N+1}{O}$ $\underset{X-4}{T}$ $\underset{D+4}{H}$ $\underset{C-2}{A}$ $\underset{Z-4}{V}$ $\underset{B+3}{E}$

$\underset{P-3}{M}$ $\underset{Q-2}{O}$ $\underset{J+4}{N}$ $\underset{G-2}{E}$ $\underset{Z-1}{Y}$ $\underset{A+5}{F}$ $\underset{K+4}{O}$ $\underset{Q+1}{R}$

$\underset{A+2}{C}$ $\underset{C-2}{A}$ $\underset{D-2}{B}$ $\underset{H-2}{F}$ $\underset{D-3}{A}$ $\underset{Q+1}{R}$ $\underset{C+2}{E}$.

answer for page 33

answer for page 34

THEY	ASKED	HIM
HEYT	DESAK	MIH
COME	BACK	LATER
MOCE	KCAB	RALTE
PICK	THEM	
IKPC	HETM	

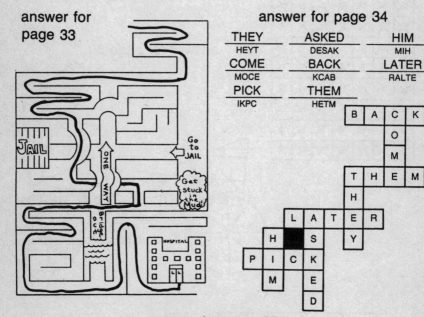

answer for page 35

60

answer for page 36

He left the men there and went home.

He had to work harder than ever.

He sold me the very next day.

He sued the men who kept him waiting.

He drove the men far out of town and made them walk back.

He nearly died.

answer for page 37

S O   O N C E   A G A I N   I   W A S   S O L D.

answer for page 38

U S E D   M E   A S   A   C A R T   H O R S E.
12 16 9 7   25 9   1 16   1   5 1 18 14   15 24 18 16 9

answer for page 39

"T H E R E'S   N O   S E N S E   I N
14 15 9 18 9 16   26 24   16 9 26 16 9   17 26

M A K I N G   T W O   T R I P S   I F
25 1 21 17 26 13   14 8 24   14 18 17 22 16   17 11

O N E   W I L L   D O."
24 26 9   8 17 23 23   7 24

61

answer for page 40

$$\underset{14}{S}\ K\ \underset{28}{I}\ \underset{3}{N}\ \underset{39}{N}\ \underset{42}{E}\ \underset{32}{R}$$

answer for page 41

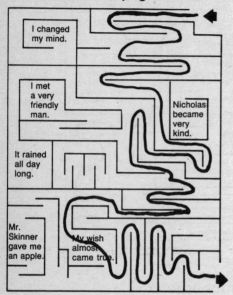

I changed my mind.

I met a very friendly man.

Nicholas became very kind.

It rained all day long.

Mr. Skinner gave me an apple.

My wish almost came true.

answer for page 42

T H E   S P R I N G S
S A G G E D.

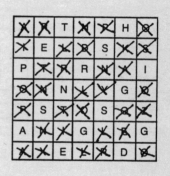

answer for page 43

I FELL TO THE GROUND.

62

answer for page 44

<u>S</u> <u>E</u> <u>L</u> <u>L</u>   <u>M</u> <u>E</u>.

answer for page 45

" <u>GRANDFATHER</u>,
  DRANGHERFAT

<u>YOU</u>   <u>CAN</u>
 OYU   NAC

<u>MAKE</u>   <u>HIM</u>
 AKEM   MHI

<u>YOUNG</u>   <u>AGAIN</u> ,"
 ONYGU   INAGA

answer for page 46

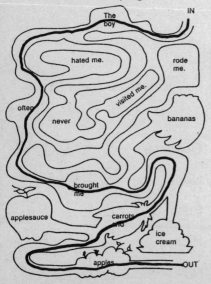

answer for page 47

$\underset{O}{\underline{B}} \underset{L}{\underline{Y}}$ $\underset{F}{\underline{S}} \underset{C}{\underline{P}} \underset{E}{\underline{R}} \underset{V}{\underline{I}} \underset{A}{\underline{N}} \underset{T}{\underline{G}}$, $\underset{V}{\underline{I}}$

$\underset{S}{\underline{F}} \underset{R}{\underline{E}} \underset{Y}{\underline{L}} \underset{G}{\underline{T}}$ $\underset{L}{\underline{Y}} \underset{B}{\underline{O}} \underset{H}{\underline{U}} \underset{A}{\underline{N}} \underset{T}{\underline{G}} \underset{R}{\underline{E}} R$

$\underset{G}{\underline{T}} \underset{U}{\underline{H}} \underset{N}{\underline{A}} \underset{A}{\underline{N}}$ $\underset{V}{\underline{I}}$ $\underset{U}{\underline{H}} \underset{N}{\underline{A}} \underset{Q}{\underline{D}}$

$\underset{V}{\underline{I}} \underset{A}{\underline{N}}$ $\underset{L}{\underline{Y}} \underset{R}{\underline{E}} \underset{N}{\underline{A}} \underset{E}{\underline{R}} \underset{F}{\underline{S}}$.

63

answer for page 48

SUMMER   DAY
WINTER   NIGHT

BOY
GIRL

HIS
HER

UP
DOWN

STARTED
ENDED

DOWN
UP

answer for page 49

" <u>W E</u>   <u>W I L L</u>   <u>U S E</u>

<u>H I M</u>   <u>F O R</u>   <u>A</u>   <u>F E W</u>

<u>D A Y S</u>,   <u>A N D</u>   <u>I F</u>

<u>H E</u>   <u>I S</u>   <u>G O O D</u>   <u>W E</u>

<u>W I L L</u>   <u>B U Y</u>   <u>H I M</u>."

answer for page 50

" <u>BLACK</u>   <u>BEAUTY</u> , is

<u>THAT</u>   <u>REALLY</u>   <u>YOU</u> ?"

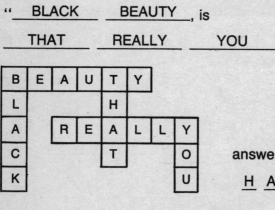

answer for page 51

<u>H A P P Y</u>.

Goodbye	Ⓗ E L L O
None	Ⓐ L L
Push	Ⓟ U L L
Rich	Ⓟ O O R
No	Ⓨ E S

64